The Covenant of Fatherhood

Apostle Courtney McLean

PUBLISHED BY:

Jamaica, W.I.

The Covenant of Fatherhood

N.B. Please note that all scripture references are taken from the King James Version of the Holy Bible unless otherwise noted.

ISBN 978 976 97035 8 2

Published by: Yahweh's Anointed Publishing

Tel: 876-549-0063/876-438-2256

Email: yahwehsanointedpublishing@gmail.com

Website: https://yapublishing.com

CONTENTS

INTRODUCTION

How can I give what I don't have? How can I embody what I have never seen? How can I accept others when all my life, what I have received is rejection? How can I heal the wounded if I have not been restored? How can I avoid damaging those entrusted in my care when I have not seen fatherhood modelled? These were the questions that went through my mind when God told me, "Son, I am calling you not just to pastor but to father the members."

As I struggled inwardly, seeking to figure out the best way to father my biological children, this extra pressure was added to father the members.

Let me be clear that I appreciate my dad and his commitment to our family. With less than a primary school education, he fought to take care of his family. He was faithful to my mother, and although he had multiple opportunities to abandon us, he stayed, seeking to raise us the best way he could. For that, I salute you, Balfour McLean, Mighty Dad of Valour, my father, a hero among men!! I learned the principles of hard work, commitment, and faithfulness from you, Dad. Thank you.

This journey is to help us embrace the

covenant of fatherhood so that we may add to the process of restoring the hearts of the fathers to the children and the hearts of the children to the fathers, as stated in Malachi 4:5-6.

WEEK 1

THE SIGNIFICANCE OF FATHERHOOD

DAY 1: THE CRISIS OF FATHERLESSNESS

Today's world faces a crisis of fatherlessness. Many honour and understand the significance of motherhood, but comparatively, few revere fatherhood in the same way. This unfortunate fact is felt in every aspect of our culture. Take, for instance, the emphasis many place on the average Mother's Day and compare that to the comparatively relaxed approach most bring to Father's Day. It is clear from this example alone that we are living in a situation that places little priority on celebrating fatherhood. Why is this?

It is very common today to see family situations where only the mother is represented as a parent in the household. In other family situations where both parents are present, it is also common to see where the mother alone acts as a proactive staple of the children's development. Many men are positioned to be fathers but do not seem to understand fatherhood beyond the role of being a provider. As such, their children do not recognize their father's presence in the other crucial areas of life. To make matters worse, many men today do not even adequately satisfy the role of provider, which then leaves that burden for the mother to fulfil as well. Challenges like this lead to many men feeling redundant in the family. This inadequacy leads to many fleeing the household and finding excuses or past times that give them an escape from family life. Not only do many need to understand what it is to be a father they also need to see what significance the father serves within the family.

If we were to look deeper, we would find that many men struggling in this department were not fathered themselves. In addition, in many countries, there are systems in place that contribute to making fathers seem redundant in their households. Perhaps such reasons are linked to why so many struggle to identify with God as Father, presenting a major challenge to the church because we are the children of our heavenly Father. Our mission is to win souls and shepherd them into the family of God. How can we do this effectively in a world where the role of the father is unrecognized in the family? How can we do this when even those within the church struggle to identify with a father's love?

God has given the church a mission to fulfil. Still, the mission will remain a struggle to achieve without adequately understanding the significance of fatherhood. This devotional journey was therefore created to open hearts and minds to identify the value of fatherhood. Mainly it will do this by examining the different features of God as Father and the significance of Him calling His church into covenant with Him. As we explore this, we will tackle questions like: What is a father and what is his significance? What is the significance of God being a Father? What is the significance of fatherhood to covenant? Why is fatherhood important to the church?

I hope this devotion will be a blessing to you and all those you share it with!

Meditation Guide

- What is your greatest takeaway?

____
____
____
____
____
____
____

- Do you agree that there is a crisis of fatherlessness? Why do you say so?

____
____
____
____
____
____

- What would you say is the relationship between fatherlessness and people's ability to accept God as Father?

- Meditate on the devotion and develop prayer points. Bring them to God.

DAY 2: THE FATHER WOUNDS

6 And he shall turn the heart of the fathers to the children, and the heart of the children to their fathers, lest I come and smite the earth with a curse (Malachi 4:6 KJV).

Whether you believe it or not, fatherlessness has a devastating impact on the world. According to Doctor Stephen Baskerville, fatherlessness is the most prominent factor common to every societal pathology, whether violent crimes, drug or alcohol abuse, teen pregnancy, or even suicide. Fatherlessness is at the centre of them all.

Good fathers play a crucial role in the healthy development of children. The father strengthens your sense of identity, their affirmation significantly improves your confidence, the emotional security they provide improves your self-esteem and the moral example they set opens your heart to accept the character and person of God more readily. This is not only true for biological fathers but spiritual fathers as well. Many of us, in some way or the other, have been hurt by our fathers. This hurt could have originated because of neglect, negligence, ignorance or because of some abuse done to you. Regardless of the exact source, when fathers do not assume their God-given calling to raise their children, wounds develop in our hearts that negatively affect our character and our life.

Proverbs 4:23 reminds us to guard our hearts diligently, for out of our hearts flow the issues of life. This verse tells us that many of the problems you and I face are due to the condition of our hearts. Therefore, when your heart is wounded, the issues you will deal with in life reflect those wounds. There is no doubt that God wants to do great things through the church, but those things will be hampered if the hearts of the people are not healed. To operate effectively with God, we must trust Him with all our hearts (Proverbs 3:5-6), but trusting God becomes a challenge when our hearts are wounded.

Trusting God as Father becomes even harder for many of us because we wonder how we can trust the Father we cannot see after being wounded by the fathers we do see. We struggle to receive the love of the heavenly Father because the only model of fatherhood many of us know is one of emotional neglect and abuse. It is sad that even in the church, people struggle to accept spiritual fatherhood because pastors are not seen as loving. Instead, they are viewed as distant, cold, unsociable and emotionally unavailable. As a result of these things many Christians seek to have an authentic relationship with God but it just seems out of their reach.

The prophecy of Malachi 4:6 was fulfilled in the form of John the Baptist. John came to earth in the spirit of Elijah with a mandate to restore fatherhood. He came to turn the heart of the fathers to their children and the heart of the children back to their fathers. Jesus would come eventually as the reflection of the heavenly Father. Still, John had to seek to restore the order of God in preparation for Jesus' arrival. The Bible tells us that Jesus came among his own and his own knew him not (John 1:11). John had to prepare the people because if the people were alienated from the love of their earthly fathers, they would likewise fail to identify with their heavenly Father.

After reading this, you may be aware that you, too, have wounds. You may have lived with these so long that you think they are a part of your identity. You may have grown to embrace them as a part of yourself. Hear my loving warning: you will never be able to have an authentic relationship with your heavenly Father until those wounds are healed. This is a process that takes time but it can be achieved. Start the process today by presenting your heart to God and asking Him to reveal the father wounds that you have stored up. Ask Him to give you the strength to forgive the fathers who may have hurt you. Ask Him to give you the grace to open up your heart to Him fully so that you can have an authentic relationship with Him. Ask Him to provide you with the courage to trust again. Ask Him to open your eyes to see what the true love of a true father looks like. Ask Him for the ability to embrace that love fully.

Meditation Guide

- What is your greatest takeaway?

____

____

____

____

____

____

- Do you detect evidence of any father wounds in your life?

____

____

____

____

____

____

____

____

____

____

____

____

- How has father wounds affected your ability to embrace your heavenly Father?

____

____

____

____

____

____

____

____

____

____

____

- Meditate on the devotion and develop prayer points. Bring them to God.

____

____

____

____

____

____

____

____

____

____

____

____

____

____

DAY 3: AHAB, JEZEBEL AND THE ORPHAN SPIRIT

[5] A father of the fatherless, and a judge of the widows, is God in his holy habitation. [6] God setteth the solitary in families: he bringeth out those which are bound with chains: but the rebellious dwell in a dry land (Psalm 68:5-6 KJV).

The world as we know it today is in a state of disorder. This disorder starts in the family and extends to the wider society and even to the church. God set up the institution of the family as the first government here on earth. The two main authorities in the family are the father and the mother. Of these two authorities, God has chosen the father to be the leader. As the leader, the father is the main authority chosen to represent God in the household. It is therefore the father's responsibility to govern his family within the order of God. In other words, the father is chosen by God to be the priest of his house.

Though God has called men to be leaders and priests in the family, we notice today that there has largely been a role reversal. Many men are not operating as leaders or priests, and as a result, many wives have been put in a position where they seek to fulfil the role of leader themselves. For this reason, it has become common in families to see ruling matriarchs and weak, passive, and displaced men. Sadly, this is so even within the church. These conditions give room for the operation of three evil spiritual forces, namely: Ahab, Jezebel, and the Orphan spirit.

Many men have become influenced by the spirit of Ahab. They have neglected their priestly duties and have become complacent, indifferent and weak. This creates a power vacuum within the family that needs to be filled, or else the family is at risk of falling apart. When there is no strong father, women and children are left vulnerable and as a result of this, they realize that if they are to survive, they must take matters into their own hands. This battle for survival breeds mistrust, rebellion, and a refusal to submit to authority. Eventually, without even noticing or desiring it, women and their children become open to the spirit of Jezebel. This wicked spirit is manipulative in nature and seeks to establish total control. Women tend to emphasize security for their children and themselves as a major priority, but where men have failed to provide this, the spirit of Jezebel is given the opportunity to enter as a substitute. As a result, though this spirit can target either men or women, it tends to identify with women who feel let down by the fathers in society.

Where fathers no longer stand as God's priests in the household, an opportunity is created for an orphan spirit to come upon the children. This spirit sits on those who exist in an environment of insecurity because there is no father to provide any strong sense of reassurance. As God's priests, fathers provide this sense of security through affirming their children and helping them to grow into their God-given identities. In addition, fathers also exist to provide an inheritance for their children as well. In providing this, fathers pattern what the love of God is like. When children know this from experience, it should not be difficult for them to grow up to appreciate and identify with the love of our heavenly Father. Unfortunately, this is not the case for many people because where there is Ahab, Jezebel follows and where there is Jezebel there will be those affected by the orphan spirit.

When these three spirits are in operation, the order of God is obstructed and the priesthood is rejected. The order of God must be restored because without it, certain blessings cannot flow in the life of the family. The church is God's family, but even within the church, this spiritual struggle exists. Restoring that order of God will not happen overnight but it can be restored over time as we commit to lovingly share the word of God to those who need it most. Many hearts are wounded because of the absence of true fathers, nevertheless Psalm 68:5-6 remind us of a God who is neither neglectful nor distant from those who are fatherless. He is willing to draw those who feel orphaned into His own family and is prepared to give security to those who feel like they have to go through life's struggles alone. Many people do not recognize the love of God themselves but we, as His church, can extend His love to others by carrying His heart. The challenge, however, is that for us to do this effectively for outsiders, we must be prepared to get it right at home first.

Today I speak to the orphan, the hurt, the betrayed, the rejected, disappointed and abused. God wants to love you as a father, but you must give Him that opportunity. Will you open up your heart to Him? Will you give Him the chance to show you the love of a father?

Meditation Guide

- What is your greatest takeaway?

____

____

____

____

____

____

____

____

____

____

- Does this devotion speak to you personally? How so?

- Has this devotion affected your understanding of the significance of a father's love? How so?

- Meditate on the devotion and develop prayer points. Bring them to God.

DAY 4: THE PATTERN SON

12 But as many as received him, to them gave he power to become the sons of God, even to them that believe on his name (John 1:12 KJV).

We have been exploring the significance of fatherhood, but now we must ask: what does it mean to be a son? In the traditional sense, we use the word son to refer to the male child of his parents. This is the natural definition, but that is not how sonship will be spoken of here. Spiritually, being a son mainly speaks to being a reflection of the father. In other words, being a son speaks to spiritual maturity.

When we first accept Christ as Lord and Saviour, we are given the spirit of adoption, which establishes us as children of God (Romans 8:15). After being born again we start off as babes. As new babes we start off struggling to walk in the Spirit because we have not yet gained the appropriate strength. As such, we start off creeping before we can walk. Before a baby becomes a toddler, it is normal for them to stumble time and again as they attempt to walk like their parents. It is normal for a babe to not be able to handle adult food. It is normal for a babe to puke on themselves and to pee their diapers. On the other hand, it is not normal for adults to behave like babes.

In the kingdom of God, you are expected to grow up. Though we may start as babes, we must eventually graduate to becoming children and though we are children of God, we must eventually seek to become Sons of God. Jesus did not give us power to remain children of God. He gave us power to become Sons of God. A baby is celebrated merely for its attempt to walk but the adult is celebrated by his ability to walk well. Eventually, **attempt** has to become **ability**. It is easy to forgive and restore a new convert when they fall under the temptation of certain sins, as this is merely the process they go through until maturity. The same cannot be said for a pastor, elder or minister. This is because, as more mature children, they are inevitably held to a higher standard than babes. As mature children, God gives them the responsibility to bear that babes cannot. As such, God holds them to a greater level of accountability because their mistakes have far greater consequences not only for them but for the entire body of Christ.

Sonship is the discipline that is measured by how well we emulate our Father. Jesus was the perfect example of this because He did nothing outside of what His Father did (John 5:19). As such, He stood as a point of reference to His disciples, showing them the character, actions and person of God the Father through Himself (John 14:9). Jesus did not stay on earth with His apostles forever but in the time He was with them He gave them an example to follow after He was gone. After Jesus was gone physically, it was now up to the apostles to reflect Jesus to their own disciples in the same way that Jesus patterned the heavenly Father for them. We, too, are given this responsibility. In 1 Corinthians 11:1, Paul tells the church to follow him as he follows Christ. In a similar way, God has aligned many of us with pastors that He has raised up to emulate Himself. When we are aligned with such individuals, our responsibility is to strive to emulate the example of Christ we see in them. In so doing, we will become mature.

To remain a babe is a disservice to God's church and is truly selfish. Babes rely on adults to take care of them. You cannot sit there in church relying on others take care of you forever. Learn to pray effectively for yourself so that you can pray effectively for others. Learn to flow in the supernatural so that you can be a blessing to others. Seek to become strong so that you can be strength for another. Apply yourself to learn wisdom so that you can counsel another. The process might not be comfortable. Many times you will feel awkward along the way. Keep going anyway. Growth is difficult in the beginning, dirty in the middle and delightful in the end. We have the power to become Sons so let us make a fresh commitment to strive towards maturity.

Meditation Guide

- What is your greatest takeaway?

- Based on this devotion, what does sonship mean to you?

- Why would you say that sonship is important in the body?

- Meditate on the devotion and develop prayer points. Bring them to God.

DAY 5: MANY INSTRUCTORS BUT ONE FATHER

[15] For though you might have ten thousand instructors in Christ, yet you do not have many fathers; for in Christ Jesus I have begotten you through the gospel (1 Corinthians 4:15 KJV).

There are many who misuse scripture in order to come against the principle of fatherhood. For example, many love to use what Jesus had said in Matthew 23:9 to suggest that because Jesus said, "call no man your father upon the earth", we should not embrace the principle of spiritual fatherhood. As a result of this, many people are uncomfortable with the very idea of referring to pastors as fathers.

The first problem with this stance is the issue of failing to properly divide the word of truth. Specifically, people who use this verse to discount fatherhood fail to read Jesus' comment in context. When Jesus said this it was in the context of warning the disciples not to attribute excessive honours to the hypocritical religious teachers (Scribes and Pharisees) who sought such titles because it fed their egos and made them feel that they were more important than others.

The second major problem with using

Matthew 23:9 to discount fatherhood is the fact that throughout the rest of the New Testament letters and early church history, many leaders would refer to believers in their congregation as their spiritual children and by extension, those leaders were often lovingly recognized by their congregants as spiritual fathers. In both 1 Corinthians 4:15 and Philippians 2:22, the Apostle Paul refers to himself as a father. Furthermore, in Galatians 4:19, Paul refers to the Galatian church as his children.

The danger of misusing scripture to attack fatherhood is that it cultivates an environment of familiarity, dishonour and unfaithfulness to covenant. When you align yourself with a local church you are positioning yourself to be aligned to covenant. A covenant can bless you if honoured and curse you if dishonoured. Sadly, scriptural abuses like the example above are why so many in the church are not fully benefiting from the grace that follows the ministry they have come in covenant with. They think that honouring the man of God is us worshipping him and as a result, God's representatives are often treated with scant regard by the very people who then look at God and question why certain blessings are not flowing in their life. They are not fully benefitting from the grace they are connected to because their connection is often questionable.

In 1 Corinthians 4:15, Paul has to remind the church that though they have many instructors in the faith, they only have one spiritual father. A common issue for many in the church is that they are too quick to become familiar with the grace God has connected them to. As a result, it is not rare to see such people heeding the teachings of others spiritual leaders more than the spiritual father God has directly connected them to. They honour external pastors far more than their local pastor. They have become so familiar with the set man of God that as a result, the teachings of the spiritual father have become too common for their taste. In such an environment, it does not matter how rich the grace is in that ministry or how profound the teaching is, those who are familiar will never benefit from it.

Meditation Guide

- What is your greatest takeaway?

____

____

____

____

____

____

____

____

____

- Has this devotional helped you to embrace the principle of fatherhood better? How so?

____

____

____

____

____

____

____

____

- Have you ever been guilty of becoming familiar with the ministry God has connected you to? In what ways was this so?

____

____

____

____

____

____

____

____

____

____

____

____

____

____

- Meditate on the devotion and develop prayer points. Bring them to God.

DAY 6: WEEKEND MEDITATION 1

1) In your own words, explain one reason why so many people do not understand the significance of a father.

____

____

____

____

____

____

2) How does the father wound affect our ability to have an authentic relationship with God?

____

____

____

____

____

____

3) How does fatherlessness lead to the entry of the Jezebel spirit and the Orphan spirit?

____

____

____

____

____

____

4) What are some differences between a child of God and a son of God?

5) Having read Day 5, explain in your own words what Jesus meant in Matthew 23:9.

DAY 7: WEEKEND MEDITATION 2

1) Which devotional impacted you most from week 1? Why?

____

____

____

____

____

____

____

____

2) What is the greatest takeaway from week 1?

____

____

____

____

____

____

3) How has week 1 influenced your perspective on the significance of fatherhood?

____

____

____

____

____

4) What major applications are you led to make based on the teachings of week 1?

WEEK 2
COVENANT
AND
FATHERHOOD

DAY 8: COVENANT RELATIONSHIP

[19] I call heaven and earth as witnesses today against you, that I have set before you life and death, blessing and cursing; therefore choose life, that both you and your descendants may live (Deuteronomy 30:19).

All relationships, irrespective of type, have conditions. This is because those conditions establish the nature of the relationship. No relationship can survive without observing a set of clearly defined conditions because conditions outline what is expected from each member of the relationship. In other words, for a functional relationship to be established and maintained, the rights and responsibilities of all the individuals involved must be made known. This is true for our friendly relationships, our family relationships, our professional relationships and most importantly, our relationship with God. When God calls people into a relationship with Him, He also makes known to them the conditions of that relationship. He usually does this using what is referred to as a covenant.

The word covenant, as used in the Bible, refers to an agreement, alliance, or pledge made between individuals. Covenants can take many forms and can be applied to many kinds of relationships. The highest form of covenant is a sacred agreement between God and His children.

In this covenant, God sets specific conditions, and He promises to bless us as we obey these conditions or punish us when we disobey. Deuteronomy 30:19 gives us a perfect example of what this looks like. After communicating His conditions, God goes further to tell His covenant people to obey these conditions because obedience would guarantee them life and blessing. Disobedience, on the other hand, would guarantee death and curses.

From the above example, we should see that keeping God's covenant qualifies us to receive the blessings God has promised. Likewise, this also means that when we choose not to keep God's covenant, we cannot receive the blessings He has promised. Sadly, many people do not seem to realize this. They seem to have digested a false doctrine that allows them to believe that because God is loving and merciful, they can do whatever they want and still expect God to bless them. As a result, we have churches filled with Christians who fast and pray regularly for particular breakthroughs, and they wonder why God is not answering their requests. Often, the problem is that they are focused on what they expect from God but they have not consulted God's covenant to realize what He is expecting of them. God is more than faithful and capable of delivering His side of the agreement but we must be faithful to God by delivering on our side. If we are not sensitive or responsive to God's desires, why should He be sensitive to ours? Before you put this devotional down, identify some of the stubborn issues you see in your life and ask yourself: "Am I walking in obedience to God's covenant?"

Meditation Guide

- What is your greatest takeaway?

____

____

____

____

____

____

- Do you believe that you have been walking in obedience to God's covenant? Why?

____

____

____

____

____

____

____

____

____

____

- Do you suspect that there are any difficulties in your life that exist because you have violated God's covenant?

- Meditate on the devotion and develop prayer points. Bring them to God.

DAY 9: THE BLESSING OF ABRAHAM

13 Christ hath redeemed us from the curse of the law, being made a curse for us: for it is written, cursed is everyone that hangeth on a tree:

14 That the blessing of Abraham might come on the Gentiles through Jesus Christ; that we might receive the promise of the Spirit through faith (Galatians 3:13-14).

We know from Genesis chapter 3 that God cursed the earth after mankind rebelled against Him. The earth as we know it is still operating under that curse. This curse affects every aspect of our earthly life. Through this curse comes disease, affliction, hardship, poverty and every other form of earthly suffering we experience. Though God did not revoke the curse, He did make provision for us to be delivered from the curse. He did this by forming a covenant with Abraham, through which He promised to bless all the families of the earth. This promise was ultimately fulfilled with the arrival of Jesus Christ because, through faith in Him, we have been given access to the blessings of Abraham. In so doing, he has also redeemed us from the curse.

This is great news. Therefore, every child of God should be walking in the victory of that redemption. Why, then, do many Christians struggle ceaselessly against the curses that we are supposed to be redeemed from? The reason is that many do not know how to walk in this redemption. The blessings of Abraham are not activated automatically when we accept Jesus as Lord and Saviour. To benefit from the blessings of Abraham, the promises need to be appropriated. We appropriate the promises by fully accepting God's covenant. In order to do this, we must understand that redemption needs to be **accessed**, **channeled**, **established,** and **maintained**. Truly accepting a covenant with Jesus requires us to engage these four mediums.

1) **Covenant with God is accessed through Jesus Christ**. Galatians 3:14 reminds us that the blessing of Abraham might come on the gentiles through Jesus Christ; that we might receive the promise of the Spirit through faith. The usage of the word might suggest that the blessings of Abraham are not an automatic guarantee. Though the blessing of Abraham is available for all people to access, not everyone will access it. Why is this so? This is so because there is a key condition that needs to be satisfied first. This key condition is that we can only access the blessing of Abraham through faith in Jesus Christ. You do not receive the promise simply because you want it. If you do not have faith and have not accepted

Jesus Christ, you do not qualify to benefit from the promise.

2) **Covenant with Jesus Christ is channelled through His church**. The church is the instrument through which God channels His covenant to the world. We are the body of Christ and so we carry Jesus to the world. We are the medium through which men know and become a part of God's covenant.
3) **Covenant with God is established through fatherhood**. Wherever there is fatherlessness, you can see it clearly as where there is an orphan spirit, it impedes the fulfilment of the covenant. The truth is that though many of us have been hurt by fathers, we still need the restoration that comes through fatherhood.
4) **Covenant with God is maintained through your fellowship with the saints**. There are those who think that as long as they have Jesus, they do not have to deal with other people, and as such, they avoid fellowship with the family of God. Many use the excuse that church people are too wicked; whilst excluding themselves from that accusation. The accusation generally comes from a misguided self-righteousness. The church is not a place for perfect people, but it is a place for people on a journey towards perfection. That

journey is not in isolation, but rather, it is a journey that takes place alongside a community. Though people are difficult to deal with, we need them in order to develop maturity.

Meditation Guide

- What is your greatest takeaway?

____

____

____

____

____

____

____

____

- Do you believe that you are fully honouring God's covenant? Where do you see yourself falling short?

____

____

____

____

____

____

____

____

____

____

- Is there an application you are led to make in order to walk more faithfully in God's covenant?

- Meditate on the devotion and develop prayer points. Bring them to God.

DAY 10: THE PRIVILEGES OF COVENANT

3 According as his divine power hath given unto us all things that pertain unto life and godliness, through the knowledge of him that hath called us to glory and virtue (2 Peter 1:3 KJV).

One of the major reasons for reading the Bible is to familiarize ourselves with the promises of God, which we should have access to as children of God. If God is our Father, we are therefore heirs to His kingdom (Romans 8:17). Therefore, there are certain things we should have access to simply because of our relation to Him. In fact, there are certain things Christians often pray for that ought not to be prayed for but rather accessed by demand.

It is common today for Christians to pray for the sick to be healed when in reality, God is expecting us to use our authority to command the sick to be healed. God can expect this from us because He has given us that authority to do it as his disciples. Isn't it interesting how there is no mention in the gospels of Jesus ever praying for the sick to be healed? Instead, we see where He just commanded them to be well. Sometimes He said nothing at all but just touched the sick, and they received healing. In Matthew 10:8, Jesus gave His disciples the instruction to heal the sick and cast out devils. Note that he never instructs them to pray for the sickness to leave. Nothing is wrong with us praying for each other, but we must also remember that there are certain things that we ought to have access to as people who are in covenant with God.

The truth is that God is good to all men without partiality; however, we must understand that our covenant relationship with Him makes us peculiar from regular men. Hence, there should be certain exclusive privileges accessible to people who have chosen to be in covenant with God. We know by now that covenants have conditions that dictate the rights and responsibilities of all the parties involved. Therefore, to know our rights, we must know the covenant we have agreed to. The problem for most children of God is not that they don't have rights in the kingdom but rather, they often do not know what those rights are. In 2 Peter 1:3, we are told that all things pertaining to life and godliness have already been given to us through God's divine power. Therefore, our struggle should not be to gain all things because God has already freely given us all things. Our responsibility is to access these things through gaining knowledge of the one who has called us to glory and virtue. Said simply, we are given all things by the power of God, but we access these things through knowing God.

In Hosea 4:6, God said that His people are destroyed because of their lack of knowledge. When we forget our God and His covenant, we are doing ourselves a gross injustice. When we reject God's knowledge, He likewise rejects us from His priesthood (Hosea 4:6). People tend to think that eternal life begins after we have transitioned from this life into the next, but in John 17:3, Jesus reminds us that eternal life is actually to **know the true God and Jesus Christ**. This is why, after accepting Christ as Lord and Saviour, our greatest priority is to seek intimacy with him because only through that intimacy will we be able to truly understand whom he has called us to be and what he has given us free access to. Therefore, let us do as Jesus commands in Matthew 6:33 and seek first the Kingdom of God because only after we do this can we expect "all things" to be added to us.

Meditation Guide

- What is your greatest takeaway?

____

____

____

____

____

____

____

____

- Do you truly believe that you have made knowing God your first priority? If no, what can you do differently?

- Based on this devotion, what is one major reason it is important to know God's covenant?

- Meditate on the devotion and develop prayer points. Bring them to God.

DAY 11: HONOUR GIVES ACCESS

[9] And Jabez was more honourable than his brethren: and his mother called his name Jabez, saying, Because I bare him with sorrow. [10] And Jabez called on the God of Israel, saying, oh that thou wouldest bless me indeed, and enlarge my coast, and that thine hand might be with me, and that thou wouldest keep me from evil, that it may not grieve me! And God granted him that which he requested. (1 Chronicles 4:9-10 KJV).

There are many people who struggle through life because they are fighting against burdens that others have placed on them. Sometimes these things can take the form of debts inherited from our parents or ancestors. Other times, we suffer because of the consequences that follow the poor decisions made by those around us. There are even situations where people find themselves fighting against evil declarations that were directly made against them.

As children of God, we should all have access to the blessings of Abraham, but depending on what we are fighting against, our living experience can feel as though the heavens are locked shut over our heads. It is common to see Christians gain a degree of freedom after accepting Jesus but realize soon after that there are still things frustrating the full manifestation of the blessings of Abraham in their lives. The issue here is not that God doesn't have the power to set us free but rather that we often lack the knowledge of how to access that freedom.

In 1 Chronicles 4:9-10, we are introduced to a man known as Jabez. We are told that this man was given his name because of the pain he caused his mother during her pregnancy. In fact, the name Jabez literally means, "he will cause pain". In her distress, his mother placed a label on her child that negatively affected his life. Though Jabez likely went through much hardship growing up, he still maintained his faith in God. Often, when people go through similar struggles, their hearts become wounded and their faith gets shipwrecked.

At the same time, there are people like Jabez who have been through hardships, but instead of going away from God, decided to go to God. Jabez went to God in prayer, and based on the content of his prayer, it is clear that Jabez knew God's covenant. Despite being considered cursed, Jabez knew he had an inheritance in the promises God gave to his ancestor, Abraham. In the end, God answered that prayer and eventually, the man that was once considered cursed became so blessed that a city was built in his name (1 Chronicles 2:55).

There are many who go through what Jabez has gone through, but their prayers have gone unanswered. What, then, made Jabez so special? The simple answer was that Jabez was a man who knew honour. In fact, 1 Chronicles 4:9 tells us plainly that Jabez was **more honourable** than his brethren. It's not that his brothers weren't honourable, but Jabez was **more honourable** in proportion and quantity. In other words, Jabez honoured God in a way that distinguished him from everyone else.

We know that God can do the impossible. We know that He is all-powerful and can do just about anything He wills. We also know that He is a God that upholds covenant. The question is never: "Can God deliver but rather will He deliver?" God can honour your prayer but He does not have to if you do not honour Him. In 1 Samuel 2:30, we are reminded that God honours those who honour Him and lightly esteems those who hate Him. Just because there are covenant blessings stored up for you does not mean you get them automatically. You still have to access the blessings. Honour gives you access. God is touched by your infirmity; He hears your cries but only honour moves Him to respond. Many people want deliverance. They know the promises of God and quote them in prayer regularly but few realize that just knowing the covenant without honour does not guarantee access to the promise.

Meditation Guide

- What is your greatest takeaway?

- Have you seen where honouring God has blessed your life? Why or Why not?

- Is there anything that you want to be delivered from? What applications can you take from the example of Jabez to appropriate that deliverance?

- Meditate on the devotion and develop prayer points. Bring them to God.

DAY 12: OFFENCE COMETH

[6] And blessed is he, whosoever shall not be offended in me (Matthew 11:6 KJV).

OFFENCE HURTS. There are many people out there who have abandoned God's covenant community because of offence. After being offended, what usually follows is that the offended person stops going to church as frequently, then they become more isolated from the fellowship, disconnected from the activities of the ministry and soon after they leave either the church or the faith altogether. This is not an uncommon thing. Getting offended in church is as common as getting wet in the rain. It is one thing to be offended by a church member, another thing to be offended by a leader in the church and yet another thing to be offended by God Himself. We often think that if people offend us we can run from them and go to our heavenly Father for comfort. Running to God is a good principle. The problem arrives however, when our heavenly Father offends us too. How do we run from Him and who do we run to instead of Him?

Many people today feel as though they have a right not to be offended. They especially think this way when it comes to church. The reality, however, is that it doesn't matter who you are or where you are from, other people will do something to cause you to be offended. They will do things that will hurt you both intentionally and unintentionally. You cannot control whether offence comes, but you can control how you respond to it.

"Church hurt" is a common term used to describe the offence that people experience before falling away from the church. All offences are not equal. Sometimes traumatic things happen to people inside the church that justifies their decision to leave a particular community. There are some situations where a person's choice to leave is literally a matter of life and death, heaven or hell. These extreme situations are relatively rare, however, and are usually not the dominant reasons as to why people break covenant. Often, the alleged offence takes the form of discipline or correction from the pastor or a leader. On other occasions, the source of the offence is far more mild and is something that could have been resolved had the response of the person been one of humility and love. In fact, it is easy to see that outside the church, the same offences would occur, but the offended person would respond quite differently. Worse offences happen at school or on our job, yet we do not hear of "job hurt" or "school hurt". We get offended by supervisors and co-workers alike, but we choose to stay anyway. People love to blame the church in the name of "church hurt", but in reality, the actual reason many leave is because of their own pride and self-righteousness.

The word 'covenant' comes from a Hebrew word (*berîyth*) that means "cutting". There is no covenant without a cutting. Cutting hurts, but it is also necessary. Many church members entertain the false belief that because God is a loving father, He would never hurt them. Still, the very word of God tells us that God chastises those He loves (Proverbs 3:12). Furthermore, in John 15:2, Jesus shows us that God deals with His church the same way a good farmer deals with his vine. He cuts to remove those who do not produce fruit and to purge those who do produce fruit so that they may produce more. In other words, the cutting that comes through covenant relationship is important for the church to mature properly. Covenant without cutting is a convenience and perpetual convenience corrupts good character. What is the point of the church growing in numbers if the people are not experiencing growth in character? What is the point of more people being added to the church in the name of Christ and not becoming more like Christ? Not even Jesus was exempt from offence, and He was perfect. If no servant is greater than his master, why should we be exempt (John 13:16)? No one likes to be offended, but could it be possible that God allows some of the offences we experience in order to mature us?

Meditation Guide

- What is your greatest takeaway?

____
____
____
____
____
____
____
____

- How did you think about offence before this devotion? Has this devotion impacted how you view offence? How so?

____
____
____
____
____
____
____
____
____
____
____
____
____
____
____

- Have you ever experienced offence in the church? How did you deal with it? Has this devotion influenced how you will deal with offence in the future?

____
____
____
____
____
____
____
____
____
____
____

- Meditate on the devotion and develop prayer points. Bring them to God.

____
____
____
____
____
____
____
____
____
____
____
____

DAY 13: WEEKEND MEDITATION 3

1) What is the importance of covenant in a relationship?

____

____

____

____

____

____

____

____

2) **Fill in the blank for the statements below**.

- Covenant with God is __________ through Jesus Christ.
- Covenant with Jesus Christ is __________ through his church.
- Covenant with God is __________ through fatherhood.
- Covenant with God is __________ through your __________ with the saints.

3) What is the purpose of covenant in accessing the promises of God?

____

____

____

____

4) What does the example of Jabez teach us about honour concerning covenant?

5) What are some reasons for God to allow offence in the church?

DAY 14: WEEKEND MEDITATION 4

1) Which devotional impacted you most from week 2? Why?

2) What is the greatest takeaway from week 2?

3) How has week 2 influenced your perspective on the covenant and fatherhood?

4) What major applications are you led to make based on the teachings of week 2?

CONCLUSION

I wish I could tell you that I have always succeeded in fathering my biological and spiritual children the way I should. Still, I will give myself credit for being committed to becoming the father God has called me to be, as I recognized early that society functions under the curse of an absence of fatherhood.

On a spiritual and natural level, I took steps along the journey to becoming the father I am today:

1- Accept the call to fatherhood.
I had to accept and see it as a call, even when I felt rejected by my biological and spiritual children. The emotional pain was not permitted to shift me from my position. I accepted the call, and I challenge every man, whether you have biological children or not, to know you are called to fatherhood. The Heavenly Father is our ultimate example. We rejected Him and didn't want a relationship with Him, but He pursued us. What reckless love! We are called to love the same, and love hurts.

2- Be humble and committed to learning a better way

Nightmare on 13th Street
When my first daughter turned 13, I had the most difficult season of my life. My daughter told me she's now 13 and will need more space. This statement was followed by strong rebellion and defiance.

Was a high-handed approach going to work? No, it wasn't! I had to pray and pull on the wisdom of God. I humbled myself as a pastor, a bishop, and a father and started asking questions because I was about to lose my daughter. I spoke to God, counsellors, and therapists. Eventually, I was led to read "How to Really Love Your Child." This book changed my life, and a little later, I read "Directing Your Arrows." This is a must-read! The bottom line is that the thing wasn't working, and I humbled myself to find a solution. I was willing to say I don't know, but I am committed to fatherhood, so I want to learn. My daughter, who confessed hating me, later acknowledged how blessed she is to have a father like me and that I was her best friend! Not sure I still am (I might be somewhere on the list), but that was so encouraging to hear. Part of the lesson here is to stick with it, fathers; I know it can be challenging, but press on.

3- Stop burying and blaming your past.

I believe 90% of us were wounded or damaged,

but you'll never move forward if you make excuses. Identify the wounds and scars of your past, don't ignore or suppress them. Suppression causes dysfunction. Open it up to Jesus and believe me, He will start healing. Get with a Christian therapist if you need to. It will be one of your best investments; the world needs you- you are called to fatherhood.

4. Don't abuse your power; be a servant leader.

My children have the chores of washing dishes. So, one night after communion service, I saw my daughter looking sad. I asked, "What's wrong?" She said, "It's my time of the month, I am behind with my studies, and it's my night to do the dishes." After doing all three services that Sunday, I was so tired, but I hugged her and said, "Nevermind, come, let's do them together." So, I took my jacket and shirt off and started before her. I could see the appreciation, and I got a big hug after.

Your entire journey should be towards being whole so you can give from that place. Let me give some pointers:

Affirm them. Offer emotional support and encouragement. Tell them you are special; exercise faith in them. Tell them I believe in you.

Love unconditionally. My relationship with my daughter changed when I told her I love you, and there's nothing you can do to change that. This was hard for me because when I disciplined my children, they would receive it as rejection. I had to adjust

Be committed to their success. Attend the games. If they are struggling with a subject, get them as much help as possible, and create a culture of reading for success. Reward them when books are completed, and they provide a summary. Then have discussions about the book.

Get in the mud to pull them out. Jesus came down to pull us up. I try to watch the movies they watch and then have discussions about the different world views that are being pushed and the agenda of the enemy

Be willing to apologize to your children when you are wrong. This is a big one, and you can't be too big to say I'm sorry. Even if they misunderstood me and were hurt through the process. I say, "I'm sorry that you feel that way and are going through this pain, but this is what I meant.

It takes work, but it's worth it.
Fatherhood will allow us to release world changers who are whole instead of broken and wounded people who continue a cycle of pain.

Mighty Dad of Valour Fathers
What other steps can we take as men to embrace the covenant of fatherhood and demonstrate fatherhood to our children?

About the Author

Apostle Courtney McLean is the Founder and Senior Pastor of Worship and Faith International Fellowship (WAFIF) with its head office in Jamaica and branch in Fort Lauderdale, Florida. He's truly a Visionary, having founded the WAFIF Whole Life Group of Schools including, WAFIF Christian College and the WAFIF Academy of Excellence. Apostle McLean's life message has enabled him to become a Transformational Leader and a sought-after Motivational Speaker.

Apostle Mclean is a graduate of the Andersonville Theological Seminary and holds a Master's Degree in Leadership Magna Cum Laude, and is now a Doctoral Candidate. Apostle Mclean is a Certified John Maxwell Coach, Mentor, and Speaker. He is a Master Coach, having founded the Wired to Win DNA Group of Coaches, and has certified over a hundred coaches making him one of the most highly recommended coaches and Life Coach Trainers in the Caribbean. His training is done using a comprehensive resource tool, written by him and known as the Wired to Win Productivity Planner, a portable Vision Board that gives a step-by-step approach to organizing and winning at life. He is the leader of a successful initiative called Every Man a Warrior (EMAW), a mentorship-Discipleship program where he empowers men to become exemplary leaders, husbands, and fathers. Apostle McLean oversees pastors and their churches; is an Ambassador to the United Nations, an International Chaplain, and a Lay Magistrate Association of Jamaica, St. Catherine Chapter member.

Apostle Mclean is also the Author of 'Turning Nothing into Something', Honouring God the Gateway to Success, Couples Relationship Rhythm Dashboard, What do you Believe, Every Woman a Contender (EWAC) Book 1, Lessons on Demonology Volume 1, Operation CPR devotional, Life of a Disciple Maker Devotional, the Master Key to Acceleration and Impact: Soaking in His Presence, Meditate to Elevate, Created for Impact Fasting Manual and Developing Your Prophetic Flow Manual *(for prophetic students enrolled in the School of Ministry).* He is happily married to his soul mate, Ambassador Reverend Nadine McLean and they are proud parents of 3 wonderful children, Deborah, Dominique, and Daniel.

List of Books by Author

- Honouring God the Gateway to Success
- The Life of a Disciple Maker
- Every Woman a Contender Books 1
- Every Woman a Contender Book 2
- Meditate to Elevate
- Couples Relationship Rhythm Dashboard
- The Master Key to Acceleration and Impact: Soaking in His Presence
- 5 Steps to a Winning Year
- What Do You Believe
- Developing Your Prophetic Flow Manual (for students enrolled in Prophetic school)
- Wired to Win Productivity Planner (3 months and 6 months)
- Wired to Win Executive Planner
- Operation CPR Fasting Manual
- Created for Global Impact Fasting Manual
- Turning Nothing into Something
- Turning Nothing into Something Workbook
- Wired to Win Facilitators Guide
- Wired to Win Mentee Guide

Books are available in the Amazon store

Services Offered by Author

www.ingramcontent.com/pod-product-compliance
Lightning Source LLC
LaVergne TN
LVHW010500160826
845677LV00012B/2576